# BAAL KADMON

# CHOD PRACTICE DEMYSTIFIED

## Severing the Ties That Bind

# Chod Practice Demystified
**Severing the Ties That Bind**

## By Baal Kadmon

## Copyright information

Copyright © 2017 by Baal Kadmon

All rights reserved. No part of this book may be reproduced by any mechanical, photographic, or electrical process, or in the form of a recording. Nor may it be stored in a storage/retrieval system nor transmitted or otherwise be copied for private or public use-other than "fair use" as quotations in articles or reviews—without the prior written consent of the Author.

The Information in this book is solely for educational purposes and not for the treatment, diagnosis or prescription of any diseases. This text is not meant to provide financial or health advice of any sort. The Author and the publisher are in no way liable for any use or misuse of the material. No Guarantee of results are being made in this text.

Cover

Kadmon, Baal

Chod Practice Demystified – Severing the Ties That Bind

–1st ed

Printed in the United States of America

**Cover image:** Green Tara Vector ID:85543792

Copyright:mpmpya

Book Cover Design: Baal Kadmon

At the best of my ability I have credited those who created the pictures based on the research I have conducted. If there are images in the book that have not been given due copyright notice please contact me at Resheph@baalkadmon.com and I will remedy the situation by giving proper copyright credit or I will remove the image/s at your request.

## Dedication

This book is dedicated to St Expedite and to My Patroness the Goddess Tara.

# Disclaimer

Disclaimer: By law, I need to add this statement.

This book is for educational purposes only and does not claim to prevent or cure any disease. The advice and methods in this book should not be construed as financial, medical or psychological treatment. Please seek advice from a professional if you have serious financial, medical or psychological issues. **IF A CHOD SESSION DOESN'T FEEL RIGHT TO YOU, DO NOT PERFORM IT.**

By purchasing, reading and or listening to this book, you understand that results are not guaranteed. In light of this, you understand that in the event that this book or audio does not work or causes harm in any area of your life, you agree that you do not hold Baal Kadmon, Amazon, its employees or affiliates liable for any damages you may experience or incur.

The Text and or Audio are copyrighted 2017.

# Introduction

Welcome to the second installment in the 'Baal on Buddhism' series in which I take complicated Buddhist topics and make them approachable to all. I was not initially intending on making this the second book in the series, in fact, I wasn't going to write this book until sometime in 2018. It has been on my list of books to write for several years, but an odd chain of synchronicities occurred in which pushed me to write this now.

I took it as a sign that my perspective on this practice is coming at the right time for many people. It also gave me the opportunity to reconnect with my own shadow self in the process. I keep myself to a disciplined schedule of writing, personal occult and meditation practice amongst other things. Sometimes, during this routine, certain things can be missed or fall to the side. This was an opportunity to slow down.

Chod is a very interesting practice within Tibetan Buddhism. Chod means to "Sever". It is a method of cutting through the ego so to speak. In the simplest of terms, it is a practice that allows you to release yourself from the negative effect of ego. When I say negative effects, I mean pretty much anything you may have an attachment to that is causing you pain in your life OR perhaps you are avoiding. Often, we are the source of our own pain due to unhealthy or repetitive thoughts that are driving us to lead lives mired in pain and self-sabotage. This can display itself as an addiction, a phobia or any other kind of impulsive behavior or thought that is literally driving you crazy. Often these psychological patterns can stem from childhood traumas or more likely the suppression and repression of the shadow side of the self. The Shadow, that part of ourselves that contain our hidden desires and repressed feelings. We often suppress these thoughts because they are either unacceptable or we simply want to deny that they are even there. Often, when suppressed, they cause us to lash out in a variety of ways that destroy our relationships and even ourselves. This, in time, becomes an attachment and we start to define ourselves by these very behaviors. An addict will identify themselves as addict before anything else, a person with certain dysfunctions may completely identify with it to the point that they do not realize that they have become obsessed with it. People use their dysfunction as badges and will base their entire self on these dysfunctions.

This is called an egoic attachment. We often think of ego attachment displaying itself as someone who is haughty and self-absorbed. The thing, it is that too. Ego attachment is anything that one attaches to, no matter how good or bad it might be. For example, one may be completely absorbed into spirituality that they actually become narcissists because of it. I will discuss that later in the book. That is a huge ego attachment that plagues the new age and occult circles like you wouldn't believe.

When one uses Chod, one can get to the core of their attachments and what is causing them pain and can slowly unravel it. The method may seem a bit counterintuitive since on the surface it almost appears one is fueling the dysfunction, but in fact, the opposite is occurring. We will discuss that later as well.

In this book, we will not only discuss in brief, the History of Chod and what it is. We will delve deeper into what the Shadow is and how it can drive our desires and our negative patterns in our lives. We will also discuss how we can identify residual unresolved shadow effects after a Chod practice. I like to call those hidden machinations the "hungry ghosts of the mind". And, of course, we will learn how to use Chod in a way that will make it accessible to all.

We have a lot to cover.

Let us begin.

# The What of Chod

I am often surprised that more people do not know about Chod since it is such a wonderful and helpful practice. Even friends of mine who study Tibetan Buddhism don't know about it, and if they do, it is a distant and vague knowledge. In my estimation, Chod is one of the most valuable practices to come out of Tibetan Buddhism. There are a few books on Chod available and they are quite good. Some are a bit heady and intellectual and others are more practical and even fairly self-help like. All good within the context in which they are written. I am going to jump in and see if I can make it even more accessible. I will even add a few new aspects not present in the other books. They will be experiments in Chod as it were.

**What is Chod?**

The word Chod means to "cut off" or "to slay" or simply "sever" as I mentioned in the introduction. Chod is a visualization practice that can be utilized to alleviate and destroy egoic attachments. I will get into detail as to what that is later. These egoic attachments are the root of all our suffering. They display themselves in so many ways; such as destructive behaviors that we can't break free of, neurotic and compulsive thoughts and feelings that are destroying us from within, just to name a few.

In Chod, these attachments are often referred to as demons, we will also discuss the various demons in a later chapter. For now, we are going to go over the basics.

In traditional Chod, the practice is usually performed in a grave yard or cremation ground. This is to challenge the ego and its fears. It's very similar to certain Shaivite Hindu sects who meditate in cremation grounds so as to eradicate the egoic attachments by reminding themselves that life is transient and therefore, attaching to anything of this world, including the body, is futile since it will perish one day.

In Chod, via a rather intense visualization that can be different with each tradition. In a popular version of Chod, an individual turns their physical self into a liquid nectar that is then fed to the egoic attachment or demon. In essence, you are feeding this demon. It may seem counterintuitive, one would think that you would want to starve the demon. But, in fact, the demon is causing you all these issues BECAUSE it is starved. If you give the demon what it needs, it loosens its hold on you. You want a satiated demon so to speak.

There are many meditations and visualization scenarios one can use to perform Chod. Above I used a tame version of Chod in which we become nectar. There are other ways to perform Chod as well. A more primal and truer to the original version of Chod is to visualize one's self being torn to shreds by animals or demonic spirits. This is to remind us as to how fragile our body is. In this process, you then offer these pieces of yourself to your fears. You are essentially facing your fears in order to immunize yourself from the attachments they cause. We are, in essence, facing our adversity head-on. As the "Mother" of Chod, Machig Labdrön said, "To consider adversity as a friend is the instruction of Chod." I will discuss Machig Labdron in the next chapter.

Please keep in mind, as I hinted at above, these demons are not demons in the western sense of the word. These are not demonic entities from hell. Rather, they are our fears and attachments and all those thoughts and ideas that we hold on to for dear life. These ideas and thoughts almost seem to have a life of their own. Through the ego, they create an artificial divide from the self or one can say our true essence. This divide causes us to develop a shadow-self that causes us harm if not tended to. I know many Buddhists will be up in arms that I am even mentioning the term "Self", since Buddhism doesn't believe in a self as we know it. However, for the sake of simplicity and approachability, I am going to use the term self since this is how we experience it. Chod practice helps integrate these divided pieces that haunt the shadow side of ourselves.

The above, of course is a very western view of how Chod works. As I indicated earlier, in Buddhism there is no such concept of "Self". Although we use Chod to release egoic attachments, Chod's ultimate goal is to release us from the egoic tendency all together by helping us ascertain the illusory nature of existence.

My friend Akasha (https://occultistakasha.com/) made an interesting observation about Chod. Not only is it a practice of severing the attachments that bind us, but it is also a way of paying off Karmic debts from a previous life. This makes perfect sense since we do carry some of the darkness with us and Chod is a way to sever that attachment. It is a brilliant observation.

In this way, Chod is an advanced practice. In this book, we will bring it a bit more down to earth so we can actually use it.

In the next chapter, we will discuss the history of Chod.

## The Who and When of Chod

Although we will be focusing on one form of Chod with a few experiments thrown in for good measure. The Chod Practice itself is very diverse. There is not one single Chod practice. Rather, there are several traditions that are tightly bound to certain lineages. There is even a Hindu Chod Tradition but for the sake of brevity, we will only discuss the ones found within Tibetan Buddhism. In Tibet, there are two main traditions often called "Father" and "Mother" lineages as they pertain to Chod. This is because there are two individuals that had the most impact on Chod. Without them, we wouldn't really know about Chod here in the west. We have the "Father" of Chod, Dampa Sangye and the "Mother" of Chod, Machig Labdron. In some circles, Dampa Sangye's roll is minimized and more emphasis is placed on Machig Labdrons contribution to Chod, some even say she was the founder of the Chod practice altogether or rather a lineage of Chod called Mahamudra. It's hard to tell who is correct. However, I too will be focused more on Machig Labdrons ideas since hers is a bit more well-known and more information is available.

Let us briefly discuss both Dampa Sangye and Machig Labdron.

## Dampa Sangye:

Dampa Sangye was born in what is now called Andhra Pradesh in Southeastern India. The exact date of his birth is unknown but it is believed to be in the 11th century. It is not clear who his parents where exactly but it was believed his father was named Viravarman, not a ton is known about him, some say he was a captain at sea or a jewel merchant. His mother, Barasaha, was from a family that made and sold incense. Not a bad business to be in at the time.

As with most figures who would later be ascribed great spiritual power, his birth was unusual. It was said that his past 7 lives, he was born a Brahmin, this is called, aptly "Seventh-Birth Brahmin".

Dampa was very learned, he was ordained at a very well-known monastery in Bihar. There, he was inundated with magickal and spiritual studies. He learned with proficiency, Tantra, the sutras, he attained several levels of Siddhi. Aside from study, he made it a habit of traveling extensively to places in which he would meditate for days on end. Essentially, he was on an every-lasting pilgrimage. These places ran the gamut. Some were very well-known temples, and some of his trips led him to remote jungle hideouts and cemeteries. This was not uncommon. Many people would flee to the jungles and cemeteries to meditate. It is said that doing so helps one reach enlightenment.

According to the Blue Annals, a Tibet religious Historic survey completed in the 1400's, states that he went to Tibet on several occasions. It was there that he picked up nicknames such as the "Little Black Indian". His first two visits were rather uneventful. Although he was, by this time, very knowledgeable, he was not able to find many students. However, upon his third visit, he was able to find some, and it was on this trip that he started to teach Chod.

He was quite progressive and had both male and female students and taught them equally without bias. He had a very interesting teaching style. Every word and movement he made had a meaning. His method of teaching was certainly very physical. This was probably quite a sight since he wore hardly any clothing and he was ascetic which indicates that perhaps he was not of robust stature. This method attracted scores of students. One thing to make note of is that much of his odd teaching style was transmitted through his student Kunga. This leads some to believe that perhaps Dampa himself did not know Tibetan.

For the most part, when people think of Chod, they think of Machig Labdron, I will cover her in the next section of this chapter. However, it is not clear who created the Chod practice.

Some say Dampa taught her the method. It is not clear if this is the case since some stories state they had only a passing acquaintance. In either case, we do know that he had a big hand in its dissemination.

## Machig Labdron:

Machig Labdron is by far the most cited person when it comes to Chod and therefore we will place more emphasis on her story. We have a lot of information about her, but unfortunately, the sources that contain this information tend to have some substantial differences in their accounts of her life. In light of this, we will need to assume that some of them may or may not be correct. There is no way for me to know, but let us see what we can discover.

It was said that she was born in the year 1055 in a Tibetan village called Tsomer. Some say she was born elsewhere, but for our purposes we will stick to one location since this is not a biographical work. Like many great teachers, the early years were remarkable. When she was born, it was said that she was an emanation of the great Mother of Wisdom and the Goddess Tara. As a young child, she was naturally drawn to Buddhism and started studying quite early. She caught on very quickly and was a great help to her teacher Drapa Ngonshe in explaining complex Buddhist concepts to other people.

It was quickly realized that she was starting to get very advanced and started to learn a teaching called Outer Cycle of Maya. I tried to find more substantial information on what these teachings are, but I could not find much and therefore I will not be explaining it here. If you do find something good, please let me know.

It was around this time she had several children. When the children got older, Machig eventually returned to her old way of teaching. She dressed like a renunciate, shaved her head and travelled wherever she could, to gain more knowledge in the Tibetan tradition. In time, she develops quite the following and started to teach. She centered most of her teaching in a cave in which she also lived.

It is said she developed the Chod practice by incorporating Dzogchen teachings with the Shamanism that was prevalent at the time. Even to this day there is quite a bit of Native Shamanism in Tibet. (Dzogchen teachings by the way are a Tibetan tradition that is meant to help the practitioner or student to discover the "primordial state of being". It is too complex to discuss in this book. However, I will write more on Dzogchen teachings in an upcoming text in this series.)

Back to Machig.

Not everyone thought she was a qualified to teach. There was quite a bit of debate as to her rights to teach at all. Buddhists from India were not so sure she had the authority to teach Buddhism that emerged from their land. Through much debate with the Indian gurus, she was later deemed an authentic teacher and her ideas were accepted. More specifically, her ideas of Chod. It became so wide-spread that it eventually was introduced to India. Chod, was, at the time the only Buddhist teaching to emerge from Tibet that made it into India. This was a big deal, since those in India could not fathom Buddhist teaching coming from anywhere else, but India. Although Chod is not widespread in India at the present time. It is there, and we have Machig to thank for this.

In the next three chapters, we will get into elements of the shadow and the subconscious mind.

Let us proceed.

# The Devils of Ego Fixation And How they Form Attachments

> "The origin of all demons is in mind itself. When awareness holds on and embraces any outer object, it is in the hold of a demon."
>
> Machig Labdron

**According to** Machig Labdron, the demons are not of a supernatural nature but within our own psyches as the quote above suggests.

In her understanding, there are four demons of attachment.

We have the demon of tangibility. This class of "demon" is based on what we can experience with our senses that can cause us discomfort, but also accounts for cravings as well. We tend to get lured into attachments by what we perceive with our senses. These tangible experiences can be either good or bad. Since both good and bad experiences can cause attachments.

We have the demon of intangibility. This is a bit trickier since these demons don't come directly from our senses, but rather what comes from our minds. Our emotions and thoughts are run by this demon; Our obsessive and negative thoughts,

thoughts of worthlessness and dissatisfaction. Our judgments of others and ourselves also come from this demon. This, in many ways is the most dangerous of demons since it is through our emotions and mental self that we navigate the world. I have found that most people who use Chod are having difficulty with this demon. Often the tangible and intangible demons show up together since many of the negative emotional traumas are due to physical traumas and experiences in the world. As I stated a moment ago, these tangible and intangible experiences can be either good or bad. Since both good and bad experiences can cause attachments.

Next, we have the demon of Exaltation, which is in many ways tied to the demon of intangibility we just discussed. This demon is also tricky because in our western conception, what this "demon" does is actually a good thing in our minds. This demon forms attachments to things that provide us a lot of joy or bliss. Instead of experiencing those things in the moment, we get attached to them. For example, I have a friend who does intense Yogic meditations every morning. She gets so intoxicated by the energy she experiences that she can't go a day without it. In our western mind, this is a great thing. We think, it's better than taking drugs, right? Well, no, it's about the same when looked through the lens of the demon. If an attachment develops, to the "good feeling" or "bliss" of whatever it is that elicits it, is considered an attachment. So as in the example above, if my friend misses her meditation sessions for a day, she is irritable and angry. SHE MUST HAVE IT. Another sign that she is too attached is that she often feels superior to those who do not meditate. The child of such an attachment is called "spiritual narcissism". That, my friends is an attachment, and we know this because if you feel any pain when you don't foster the attachment, that means you are addicted to it and that is a strong attachment. Are some attachments worse than others? I suppose, but they are all pretty bad because they cause withdrawal when they are not fostered. Chod can help break these attachments.

The next demon is also very connected to the last demon we just discussed and that is the demon of arrogance. There is just a small twist to this one. Although it incorporates many of the elements of the prior demon, it goes a bit deeper. Not only does this demon tend to be present with inflated egos and spiritual narcissistic tendencies, it also makes you believe that you are an autonomous self. Let me explain, unlike Hinduism in which there is a self. In Buddhism, the self is non-existent and therefore if you even have an inkling of autonomy or individuality, you are delusional. This feeling of "identity" is considered to be of the highest form of arrogance. When one pacifies this demon, you can then realize your true pure state which is grounded in the emptiness of all that is. You start to realize that everything we experience is diaphanous and has no intrinsic meaning. I know, this demon is a hard one because it is almost impossible for us to look in the mirror and think that there is really not much to us. Or when we speak to others, we look at them as if they are a person with a name. It's so hard because our senses tend to take things that are being experienced as being the end-all-be-all of the sensation. If I smell perfume, my nose is detecting this but in the overall scheme of things that was an illusion since the whole scent and sense are experiencing aspects of a "universe" that doesn't exist in the proper sense of the word. Even this explanation I am giving you is an experience and doesn't really describe something that can't be described. And even those words are illusions. Essentially, the use of labels of any kind will trap you in this demon. To say there is no self, would acknowledge that there is a self to compare against it. You see what I mean? You can't know dark without light, yet both aren't TRULY real. You see the rabbit hole you jump down into when you discuss these concepts? Oh, and, that rabbit hole isn't really either, but even saying that isn't true. It's quite maddening, at least to the logical mind.

Now that we have that out of the way, let is go a bit deeper into the subconscious mind and some of its tendencies since it is this part of the mind where attachments form.

## The Subconscious Mind

For as long as humanity has been on this planet, we still know very little about the world outside of us. We certainly know more as time goes by, but even the most expert in any field will tell you that we are only truly beginning to understand most of what we experience as humans. Same is true for our inner world as well. Especially that aspect of mind we call the subconscious.

The subconscious mind is largely a mystery to us, it's a mysterious and dark place. It contains all our inner secrets and desires. It is also is the repository of all our highest aspirations. When spirit interacts with us, it is often channeled through these mysterious subconscious corridors of our mind. It truly controls most of our life; a good 90% of our daily existence is being run behind the scenes in this murky place. Despite this, we can see its influence and even control how it works on some limited level. Since it controls much of our life, its finger prints are everywhere.

The subconscious mind has several characteristics that we can easily ascertain. I will go into six of them. There are many more, but for our purposes and understanding, I will just mention these.

- Anything you are not actively controlling in your mind is being controlled by it.
- It has a photographic memory
- Despite outward appearances, it is trying so very hard to protect you from emotional pain and damage.
- It views the waking and dream world as one and the same.
- It will always get its way unless you snap out of your default state.
- It is a habit making machine and its specialty is consistency.

**Anything you are not actively controlling in your mind and body is being controlled by it.**

Everything in your mind and body is controlled by the subconscious mind, thus it is actively controlling everything you are not consciously controlling. This fact alone is testament to how powerful this part of your mind is. If you could tap into even a fraction of this part of your minds power, it would revolutionize your life.

Unfortunately, not everything it controls is necessarily good for you. Addiction, for example, is not just a physiological issue but a subconscious mind issue as well. The Subconscious mind, although the repository of many wonderful things, it is also sort of stupid, for lack of a better term. It doesn't care what routine you create, if you continue to do something over and over again, it will make sure to make it a habit and will warp your thoughts, so you can rationalize those habits. Some of these habits then can become addictions. Of course, some habits are good as well, such as the obvious ones like brushing your teeth etc. It essentially takes an action that is at first under your conscious control and then makes it unconscious. As you see, not all these automated actions are always good. All of our self-sabotaging ways can often find its roots in this function of the Subconscious mind.

## It has a photographic memory

You may not remember everything consciously, but your subconscious mind is remembering every single thing you are doing and everything you are experiencing. It uses several parts of the brain for this. When it comes to our fears, we have Cortex memory, which is that front part of our brain that is also known as the "executive brain". This part helps us analyze ideas and events etc. When it remembers traumatic events, it does so in a way that affects the thought process as a whole. For example, let's say you text or call your boyfriend or girlfriend and they don't answer. At first you are fine, thinking they are busy. After a few more attempts, you start fearing that either something happened to them OR perhaps they are cheating on you etc. You may think this because, perhaps, you were cheated upon once before and that left a scar. Later you find out they forgot their phone at home or the phone ran out of charge. But you see? Instead of thinking those things, your executive brain thought the worst, and notice how automatically it did so. That's your subconscious mind pushing those thoughts to the forefront.

Now, there is another part of the brain the subconscious mind uses that is often useful, but also can malfunction due to trauma. The Amygdala, this part of the brain prompts our flight or fight response in the face of danger. This, of course, is good in many cases. You see a rabid dog running after you, you aren't about to run to it and give it a belly rub. You are going to run like hell. That impulse to run will be directed by the Amygdala. Now that this part of the mind has recorded this frightening event, it can either store it for the future in a way that will protect you OR it can also malfunction. An example of malfunction is the sudden fear of all or most animals OR the fear of all dogs. I recall once I got bitten by a dog on the hand in the early 2000s. It hurt a little bit, I was more jolted by the unexpected nature of the bite. Dogs love me, so it was a bit odd. From that moment onward, when I saw dogs that didn't belong to me, I automatically avoided them, and I didn't even think about it. You see? That is irrational, not all dogs will bite me, but the event was sufficient to create a memory in the Amygdala that malfunctioned and became a generalize fear and response. So In essence, you can tell the difference between a Cortex memory and Amygdala memory of a traumatic event by the way it displays itself. If it involves a lot of thought and rumination, it is most probably a cortex memory and if it is more instinctual, it's most likely an Amygdala memory.

Both these memory types create blockages in our mind and energy field that we need to heal, Chod can help with this. We will get into that a bit later in the book.

## Despite outward appearances, it is trying so very hard to protect you from emotional pain and damage

As I stated in the section above, this memory can display itself in several ways. I used examples in which these memories can malfunction. In this section, I will explain why this malfunction occurs. As I mentioned, the Subconscious tries very hard to protect you from negative events and it does so via the memories it creates in the various parts of the brain. Despite it malfunctioning from time to time or even often, the intention of the fears and blockages is not actually a bad one. It simply gets a bit out of hand. The subconscious mind, when it perceives a threat will bring a nuclear bomb to a knife fight.

For example, if you went through a hard breakup, the pain of such an event can often make it hard for you to get into relationships in the future. This fear is understandable, who wants to get hurt? On the other hand, if you let it guide you, you will never again enjoy the feelings of being in a relationship. This fear can get to the point where it becomes crippling. When this fear is allowed to stew, it plays tricks on the mind.

These tricks are so covert that you don't even know they are occurring. They show up as defense mechanisms in the mind. As the word implies, they are defensive in nature. The subconscious mind is trying to protect you, not harm you, but it often does so in a more extreme manner. These defense mechanisms are in a sense, scar tissue. Scar tissue is actually supposed to be good because it protects the area from further trauma. The problem is, scars aren't always pretty.

As the defense mechanism remains deployed, even when the danger is no longer present, it slowly erodes the mind. Suddenly rationalizations pop up. They do so to iron out the cognitive dissonance that is created between your desire to be in relationship and the fear of getting hurt. The rationalizations although appear conscious, they are in fact unconscious processes.

**Rationalization is a powerful weapon of the subconscious mind because it is so seamlessly woven into your thought processes. You don't realize that it has hijacked your better judgment and therefore you don't know it is happening at all.**

To stay with the above scenario, one example of this rationalization might be "I am very picky" or " they aren't my type anyway, so why bother?" Don't get me wrong, certainly, there are people who are not your type, but when you find yourself saying that all the time, chances are, you might be hijacked by a defense mechanism. It is important to know this fact. Defense mechanism activation can be very much embedded into your mind and they become vehicles of attachment. Chod can help with this.

## It views the waking and dream world as one and the same

As odd as this may sound, the subconscious mind does not know the difference between the outside world and the inner one. In other words, waking and dream states are one and the same. The only time it will push back on this is when you have a deeply rooted habit of action or thinking. If, for example, you are bad with money, you can't simply say "I am good with money". It will push back on that and may even deepen your lack of financial skills. So in this way, it knows that this statement "I am good with money" is false. It is not a conscious knowing, but an automatic one. As you can see, the habit making mechanism in the subconscious mind extends to thoughts as well.

Here is a scenario proving that the subconscious mind aside from its habit-forming mechanism has no idea of what is real and what is not real for lack of a better term.

Have you ever had a dream that seemed so real that your body actually responded to it? Such as a falling dream, or a sad dream that made you cry when you woke up? Notice how the body reacted; it reacted as if it was a real event. Your subconscious mind is most "itself" when it is in the dream state and so it thinks the content of the dream is so real that it tells the body to respond as if it were an actual event taking place in waking consciousness. If it knew the difference between actually falling down and falling down in a dream, you wouldn't grip the bed as if you were falling. The fact the subconscious mind makes you react like you are actually falling is proof positive it has no conception at all of reality.

Countless studies have been done to prove the subconscious mind has no sense of reality. This aspect of the subconscious mind has been studied by Athletes, Astronauts and many more who have used this to their advantage for decades. It's has been called Visual Motor Rehearsal. it is Like a dream, but instead of being a sleep, you are consciously enacting something without actually doing it in real life, you are simply only visualizing it. It has been proven that by just using your senses to imagine yourself doing a particular sport or activity; the required muscles will start reacting as if you were really performing this activity. **The conscious mind knows full well you aren't actually performing this activity, but the subconscious mind has no clue and starts firing on all cylinders as if you were really performing the activity.**

There was an interesting study further illustrating how the subconscious mind takes much of what it filters as actual and real.

Melissa Bateson and colleagues at Newcastle University, UK conducted an experiment at their psychology departments coffee room. In the coffee room, faculty were encouraged to have as much coffee and tea as they like. This system was run using an "Honesty Box". This box collected money for the coffee and tea that was provided for the faculty. Although it was not "mandatory" to leave money, it is a courteous practice to do so.

Above the honesty box they placed a nice picture of flowers and a price list. At the end of the week, not much money was collected. However, the following week the picture was not that of flowers, but of a pair of eyes staring right at the person who happens to be in front of the "honesty box" at the time. The faces changed, but the eyes were always staring, directly at the person in front of the "Honesty box". Although the pair of eyes was just a photocopy of actual eyes the faculty reacted unconsciously to those eyes as if they were real. How do we know? The weeks that the picture of the eyes was present, more money was collected. In fact, 2.76 times more money was collected during the weeks the eyes were above the "Honesty Box". Although this study was to measure "honesty" and the various subliminal cues involved in producing honest behavior, it also illustrates to me that the subconscious mind prompts behavior based on stimuli it perceives as real. If the subconscious mind truly knew that the image of the pair of eyes was not an actual set of eyes, it wouldn't have prompted unconscious behavior indicating the opposite. This study can be found in *Biology Letters* (DOI: 10.1098/rsbl.2006.0509).

### **It will always get its way unless you snap out of your default state.**

As I mentioned, the subconscious mind loves repetition. In fact, I will repeat this fact over and over again because that is the best way to learn. This is a very critical element of the subconscious mind that we need to focus on the most. The fact that the subconscious mind always gets its way is the reason why we are often stuck in our repetitive self-sabotaging patterns. If we do not lessen this negative charge, it can sabotage our lives. Chod helps get rid of this attachment symptom.

If we do not reduce the charge, it will succeed almost every time in its efforts to derail you, especially if you have a lot of negative habits of thought and action. It always gets its way. This is why it has been historically difficult for people to change. The old program is still running, sure, it can go into the background but after a while it starts draining your resources and you will be forced to either cave into it or use it to move forward.

Often, many self-help books will tell you that the moment you have a negative thought or feel the need to self-sabotage, you must immediately think about something else. This works for a moment and may even work for a few days, but it is not a solution. After a short time the old behavior rebounds and not only does the negative emotions come back, but they often come back with a vengeance. These authors are asking you to suppress the emotion.

Here, let me show you how futile this is.

I am going to ask you to do something....

**DO NOT THINK OF A WHITE BEAR!**

Hmm, I bet you thought of a white bear, right? The reason for this is that when you try to suppress a thought, the mind will then go on a mission NOT to think of a white bear. Unfortunately, in the process, it must think of the white bear in order to avoid thinking about it. The same thing is happening when you try to suppress emotions and negative thoughts.

To consciously suppress these things is like building a dam with holes in it. Sure, it keeps most of the water out; that is until the holes get larger and the whole structure breaks apart and you are utterly swept away by the current.

So we must acknowledge that the subconscious will always get its own way if we try to resist it and fight it. Instead, we need to redirect its energy, we need to give it what it needs. When we use Chod, it helps redirect this energy, so we can use it more efficiently. For some this could have long-term positive effects and for some, it may be short term. That is why it is called a Chod practice, we must practice it in order to fully benefit from it.

**It is a habit making machine and its specialty is consistency.**

When you think about it, we are all incredibly mindless in our day to day lives. How often do you think about what you are doing or thinking at any given moment? Do you think about your thinking? Or are you on autopilot? We are all on autopilot when we go about our days and that is not a bad thing for the most part. Most of our days are consumed by fairly routine tasks, that if we had to think about them all the time, we would never get anything done. Imagine thinking about everything you do from the moment you get up to the moment you go back to sleep. Do you think about brushing your teeth? When you yawn do you think "I am yawning now"? Probably not and in those situations, it's a good thing. Habits and routines of that nature is our subconscious minds way of streamlining our lives. Like I said, imagine if even the most mundane tasks you do required constant thinking through, your life would be a misery. So in that sense, mindlessness is a good thing. But like all good things, too much of it is often NOT a good thing. The same mindlessness we go about in our day to day applies to all areas of our lives, not just those mundane tasks.

When you are worrier, you tend to carry that worry with you into each and every day. You may not even realize it. Another perfect example is anxiety, you may have pockets of calm but more often than not, if you are an anxious person, you are anxious every day and in some cases relentlessly. At this point it is so embedded into your day-to-day that you really don't know its happening. Other bad habits like eating junk food or watching excessive TV also happen by default. It is barely conscious. Come on now, you know it's true.

I'll give you an example from my own life. My late maternal grandmother used to be a worrier, and was in a constant negative state. I have no idea how she lived that way. Nothing was ever good in her world, even when things were often great. If you had a headache, she would say "maybe it's a brain tumor". If you dropped something "the devil made you do it" LITERALLY! If you coughed you either had the Flu or AIDS related pneumonia, not just a cough. If money fell out of your pocket, it was a portend of financial ruin… You get the point.

Everything that happened had a catastrophic negative connotation. So, one day, I and my brother asked her "if we were to solve all your problems and remove all the things that made you feel bad in life, what would you do?" She thought about it for what seemed like an eternity and said **"I don't know"**. She went on to say that **"misery is all she knew"**. What's interesting about her life is that it wasn't all miserable, she made it that way, but that's because it was her default state. After a while, it become a habit and a routine. It's the same thing for people who date the same kind of people over and over again or place themselves in negative situations all the time and don't understand why it happens to them.

Now, it is not all bad, optimism and good habits also get embedded in the mind and can become routine, but, well, what is interesting about our brain is that our defaults tend to be rather negatively orientated. It's for this reason it takes more time to feel better about something and only a second to feel badly about it. Light and darkness are not necessarily equal in this existence. We don't need to battle any demon or devil; in actuality those entities are more afraid of us, that is why calling upon them can be so effective. We are our own stumbling block and more often than not, we don't mean to be.

As you can see, the subconscious mind is a rather complex thing. In the next chapter, I will discuss the Shadow and how it often derails us and can often lead to self-sabotage and irrational behavior and fears. I will present an example of how this might come about.

# The Shadow Self And How It Can Manifest An Attachment – An Example

**"Everyone carries a shadow, and the less it is embodied in the individual's conscious life, the blacker and denser it is."** – Carl Jung – Psychology and Religion.

We all have a shadow, there is no way to avoid it. As we go through life, experiences start to shape who we are. I mean all experiences; from the food we eat, to the books we read and the interactions we have with the people around us. Even if we did not have any experiences at all, the shadow arises naturally from the mere fact that we are alive. In short, it is an integral part of who we are as humans.

The shadow is that part of us that is not fully known, it is the dark side of our psyche. The place where most of our negative conceptions reside. These, as I mentioned above are based on our life experiences. The shadow contains the seeds of lust, envy, greed, unresolved anger and selfishness. Its counterpart, according to Carl Jung is the conscious ego of the person. Our conscious ego is who we portray out to the world. The shadow is the unacceptable aspects of our personality that does not "jive" with who we portray ourselves to be. Because it does not fit our narrative personality, it gets repressed. This is where the problems in our lives start to form. The repression of unwanted thoughts and impulses, is the ground zero in which our destruction and our unraveling springs forth.

We can see what happens when we repress what we consider our dark sides. It is all over the news. An example of this can be found in our religious institutions. So many reside there actually. It is the pastor who preaches against drugs and alcohol and goes out of his way to shame people about it only later to be pulled over for drunk driving and a crack pipe. It is the financial manager who speaks of the importance of fulfilling one's fiduciary duty to their clients and is later found robbing his client's blind. It is the humanitarian worker trying to save abandoned children in third world countries, who is later found selling those same children as prostitutes to fulfill the craven sexual desires of pedophiles. It is the parent who badgers and abuses their child about school and demands perfection from them only to suppress the fact they have achieved nothing in their own lives.

When the shadow is repressed we easily project all our buried weakness and flaws and unacceptable emotions unto others. By denying expression of our own faults, we will project and find them in others. As long as we continue to suppress these darker thoughts, the more automatic they become. As I stated in the previous chapter, the subconscious mind LOVES repetition. It becomes, an unconscious process. Carl Jung said it best **"Until you make the unconscious, conscious, it will rule your life and you will call it fate."**

No truer words have been spoken. So how does a negative event or experience become so engrained?

I am happy you asked, let's take a look.

There are two aspects of our mind/Brain I would like to discuss that will illustrate this well.

One is called **Hebbs law**. I am sure you know of it because you have heard of its effects. It is **"Neurons that fire together, wire together"**.

When a trauma occurs in our lives, it, well, traumatizes us. Our thoughts slowly become fixated on the trauma, and understandably so. When these negative thought patterns become more repetitive, the associations in the brain get stronger. It is not unlike exercising a muscle. With each and every time you work it out, it gets stronger and stronger and even develops muscle memory. It is cumulative in nature.

This very same thing is happening in your brain as well. The neurons that are firing as you engage in this loop of thinking start to fire more and more. The connection starts to get so strong that it becomes "unconsciously controlled". It has become a routine of the subconscious mind. Since the subconscious mind "thinks" it is doing you a favor. It will continue to foster these traumatic thoughts over and over again, inflicting more damage on you, DESPITE trying to protect you.

The next concept I would like to mention is called **"The Quantum Zeno Effect."**

This one you probably know as well. It goes something like this. **"Energy flows where attention goes".**

I am sure you have heard this phrase before, it is bandied about in so many of the books on the occult and new age in general.

While Hebbs Law explains how something becomes linked in our minds; The Quantum Zeno Effect explains why this is happening.

Quantum Zeno Effect is all about how one focuses his or her thoughts and energies. It is a known fact that when you focus on something, your brain changes, certain parts light up and with time get stronger. The Quantum Zeno Effect states that when you place your focus on a thought, be it negative or positive, this very act of focusing maintains the brain state that arises in association with that experience. In other words, when you focus attention on a given experience, the circuitry in the brain that is associated with that experience remains in a very stable state. This stability then brings upon Hebbs law and the Neurons of that specific region will start firing together.

Let us look at how this might arise in a person who went through verbal abuse in his or her childhood. Let's name this person Chris.

**Life Experience**: Chris is told by his parent/s from an early age that nothing is expected of him and that he was a mistake. He is told this quite often. Since he is too young to fully process these emotions, they become small scars on his psyche. They remain small for now.

**The Subconscious Mind**: Time is going by and these thoughts are incubating in his mind. So far, they are not yet causing overt problems in his life. He hasn't been exposed to much yet, so he hasn't been fully poisoned.

**Life Experience**: An event occurs in Chris's life that reinforces his parents' words. Perhaps he fails at school, gets bullied or maybe he goes through a breakup.

**The Subconscious Mind:** So, as the subconscious mind Is want to do when a negative event occurs, it stores this negative experience in the "unworthy file". Chris is now starting to think, "Maybe my parents are right about me".

**Life Experience**: Now the mind is on the lookout for more corroborating "unworthiness" information. Whenever something goes wrong in Chris's life, he starts to link them to being unworthy. His negative thoughts begin to break out and he starts to feel pain from this.

**The Quantum Zeno Effect**: Now he is starting to entertain these thoughts more and more. The Quantum Zeno effect is now engaged, and his attention has now started to gel around thoughts of unworthiness.

**Hebbs Law:** The thoughts are now so prevalent that the neurons in his brain start firing together, this creates a deeper and deeper pathway in his brain and thus these thoughts get imbedded.

**Life Experience:** Now that he has developed this chronic negative state. He is now starting to experience events in his life that will foster this unworthiness and make it more apparent. He is the guy that always seems to have "bad luck.". He starts to self-sabotage since deep down he thinks he deserves it. These

Self sabotaging sprees cause more events to occur such as sabotaging relationships over and over again. Or perhaps making bad life choices over and over again. Or he might withdraw completely from the world because he is afraid to fuck up.

Do you ever see that person who always seems to have the same problem repeatedly? It is their "thing". The process above might be why. It's the mechanism of the repressed shadow.

The results of these moments of self-sabotage simply reinforce the cycle and the negative impact starts to compound upon itself. At this point, it may even start to invade his dreams.

Since he is now out of control and can't handle his pain, rationalizations kick in and weave seamlessly into his day-to-day thoughts which makes him feel like he isn't in need of change and that it is everyone else who needs to change. This causes Chris, despite his unworthiness issues, to judge others for their incompetence. He could be standing in a Supermarket line and silently (or not) thinking negative thoughts about the bumbling person who is slowing down the line thinking "God, this guy is worthless, he shouldn't go out if he can't get his shit together". While on the line, he might glimpse a tabloid and read about the various train wrecks occurring in Hollywood and will start to think "Wow, this person is an idiot, if I had all that money, I wouldn't be that stupid." He might see a good-looking person who may have a few pounds to lose and think "Wow, such a pretty face, too bad he/she is so fat". Meanwhile, he has about 50 pounds to lose himself. You get my point, despite his own issues, he has projected the things he hates the most about himself on others. Mind you, he is waiting in line to buy junk food and beer, not exactly edifying life choices if you ask me.

The shadow aspect in the above is in full force and has been repressed and is now running on autopilot until he actually does the work and faces the darkness. Until then, he is attached to his unworthiness. And this unworthiness will cause him to commit these acts of self-sabotage and then to assuage himself, he turns it against others to deflect from his own pain. It's a sorted business. All this is occurring so automatically at this point. You see what I mean?

This was just ONE example of how this process can work. There are many scenarios. You may even have a repressed shadow causing you harm. Perhaps it is time to use Chod to start engaging this shadow self. Let us go through a session of Chod together.

## Severing the Ties That Bind

In this chapter we will discuss the basics of the Chod practice and go through one Chod session. The template I am using in this chapter can be used for any of your Chod sessions. It is for this reason I will outline the process in generic terms.

**I must warn you, it is not always easy to encounter the issues that bind you. Some of these issues can spark some deep-seated emotions and recollections of Trauma. Please do not perform Chod if you are not ready to do so.**

I will illustrate the intent of the Chod practice and then we will get more detailed.

Create a space in your home where you will not be disturbed for about 15 to 30 minutes. You can make this longer if you like.

I personally light a candle; any color will do and light some incense. Again, you can use anything that you like. This is for ambience. If you don't like to light candles or incense that is fine too; calming music is good too. I listen to "Santosh" when I do Chod. It's a wonderful for magick and meditation.

In this session of Chod, we will be identifying the issue that is causing you pain. It can be about anything. It could be excessive shame, being too judgmental, fear of intimacy or whatever it is that is holding you back. It can be issues you have with unworthiness and everything in between.

We will then try to visualize what this pain or issue might look like. Let the image come naturally to you. It might be scary or benign looking. Just let it flow. When I first encountered my demon, it was this blue hairy monster with red eyes. It was off putting to say the least.

Once you identify the issue or "devil of egoic attachment". Call it to you, invite it into your space. Visualize it in front of you. You can do this with your eyes closed or open. If you are having a challenging time visualizing. Take a piece of paper and make a symbol that represents the issue. It can be as simple as a line or as elaborate as a drawing. Once completed, place it in front of you. Maybe on a chair in front of you so you can face it.

Once in front of you, sit with it for a few minutes. Stare at it either in your mind if you are doing a visualization or the symbol on the paper. Now ask it, in a normal tone, either in your mind or out loud.

**Please do not be afraid, come to me. I have what you desire. Please tell me, what is it that you need from me? What can I do for you?**

Let it answer you in your mind. Don't control it, let it simply answer you. If you don't hear an answer that is okay too for in the next step, we will get deeper into its energy. Once you have the answers or not. Unlike other methods in which you become the devil of egoic attachment, once I hear what it wants or if I don't hear anything, I immediately go to the next step.

The next step is a bit harsh in the sense that it requires you to do some pretty intense visualizing. It is at this point I visualize myself being cut up into pieces and my head being cut off by wild animals or demons. While I visualize this, I see the devil of egoic attachment consuming these parts of me. I let him or her eat me until there is nothing left of me. At this point I am only looking upon him as an observer now. In some books, they do away with the harsher visualizations and have you picture yourself as a nectar which is fed to the devil or demon. This is a gentler way to visual this. However, in the original Chod teaching, very harsh visualizations are used and therefore I am keeping to that tradition in this book. The harsh way shocks the ego and thus, in my mind, is more effective. If you need a gentler approach you can see yourself turning into nectar instead of being torn to shreds and this nectar is imbibed by the devil of egoic attachment.

Once the devil eats of you, you will notice it transform into something else. Mine turned into a bird. I then visualize myself and the bird become one.

It is at this point, you will notice how the emotional charge of the issue is lessened. You are no longer ignoring this lost part of you, but in fact, you are integrating it so it can't cause you harm. For persistent issues, you may find doing this a few times. Again, you can do this for whatever issues you have.

**Now let us go step by step:**

1. Sit with yourself and think of the issues that is bothering you right now. Is it shame? Anger? Whatever it is, think about it.
2. Visualize what this issue looks like. Don't control it. Just watch it and observe it.
3. Now say: **Please do not be afraid, come to me. I have what you desire. Please tell me, what is it that you need from me? What can I do for you?**
4. **Once you have the answer,** visualize yourself being cut up into pieces and your head being cut off (or nectar). While you visualize this, see the devil of egoic attachment consuming these parts of you. Let him or her eat you until there is nothing left of you. At this point, you are only looking upon him as an observer now.
5. Once you are consumed, see how this devil or demon changes form.

6. Once you see this new form, merge with it. It will be at this point when you will feel the emotional shift.

There you have it, a simple Chod session that can help you move past many of the ties that bind you. We will do other Chod sessions in which we will experiment with different entities. But before that, I do want to mention one more thing that you might experience after a Chod session. I will discuss this in the next chapter.

## Hungry Ghosts of the Mind

The demons that haunt our minds are very persistent. Sometimes when we use Chod to sever them from our lives, they linger in hidden ways. The emotional charge may dissipate but the subconscious mind has not fully rewired and so the devil of egoic attachment may still have a fingerprint on your soul. This displays itself in many ways. It is for this reason, it is imperative to continue the practice and not just stop at one session.

Let us look at three examples of how the devil of egoic attachment is still active after a session or two of Chod.

For example, a person who was sexually traumatized may have a challenging time developing close intimate bonds with another person. Or perhaps it makes them want to avoid people altogether. This is more common than you think, and it can produce intense fear when social situations arise. Such a person may perform Chod and find the emotional charge of the trauma lessens to the point that it feels like it might be gone.

This is good in the sense that heaviness of the fear is gone. However, it may still have some remanence in the mind and it shows up in such a subtle way that the person may not know it is happening. In fact, they may think this subconscious trick I will mention is a sign of progress. The person might feel free and say something like "I feel so free of the trauma and that freedom allowed me to realize, I really don't need sex or intimacy, I can live without it. " Do you see what happened there? Before they avoided intimacy out of fear, but now they are avoiding it still, but there is no apparent fear. The same exact result will occur; No intimacy or pursuit of relationships. Tricky aint it? This is a sign that more clearing needs to be done.

Let us use another relationship-based one since this is where so much trauma comes from. One of the most painful things we can go through other than the death of a loved one, is the breakup of a relationship. The bitter pain that such loss can bring can be nearly unbearable. Unless you have lived under a rock or are very young, you may not have had this experience yet. This pain, especially if experienced more than once can leave lasting scars on the psyche.

For some, when using Chod for this kind of issue may experience great release of the pain and the attachment to that pain that is causing hardship in life. I will use an example that I witnessed firsthand. One of my friends, whom I met through my facebook about three years ago, went through a devastating breakup. Her pain was so bad that she relished the thought of just jumping in front of an oncoming subway to end her life. She roamed the NYC streets like a zombie. She forgot to eat. When she got home, she would sit on her couch and literally stare at the wall, balling her eyes out. Every day she texted me and emailed me asking me for a solution to her pain. She was a wreck and I knew there was nothing I could do to help her. She had to do some inner work in order to heal. As the days went on, she started to develop a hatred for men. This is natural, I have seen this a million times, sometimes we start to have this kind of blanket hatred that allows us to rationalize our fears of intimacy. This, of course, applies to men as well as women. Our defense mechanism goes up and we suddenly see things from a warped perspective, the perspective of fear and pain.

I eventually introduced her to Chod. She needed a few sessions but she seemed to make great strides. The bite of the pain lessened with every session. But something told me that the pain simply transformed into something else... Now she no longer hated men, but now she didn't want to have anything to do with people at all. Instead of saying "people suck" she suddenly felt she didn't need anyone in her life anymore and that she only needed "God". You see what happened there? The symptoms of the trauma, like in the previous example simply changed form. The fear and pain simply put on another mask. When I told her to continue the Chod and to consider what I was telling her; She realized that indeed her pain was still there but the spiritual elements of her practice simply intoxicated her to the point that the pain changed form. It's a very sinister and covert process. The good news is, she has since made a full recovery and is ready to get back out there.

This next example is INCREDIBLY COMMON. Many of us have had some pretty hard times in life. People have hurt us and life in general can be difficult. Some of us keep moving on and realize it is part of life, whilst others become jaded from it. This jadedness causes a kind of intense dislike for people and in more extreme cases withdrawal from people and society. (I find this is VERY common in occult circles).

Chod has helped many people with this but like the other examples, more than one session will be needed. Often after a Chod session, there is a lightness in the soul. That jadedness seems to subside. However, in some, as you my suspect, experience a change of form in their initial symptoms. Suddenly they want to withdraw from people like before. But this time, it's not out of OVERT fear or jadedness but out of this grandiose idea that they are spiritually gifted and that they no longer need people. All they want to do is meditate and pray. That alone is not the problem; I encourage meditation, prayer and ritual. It's the mindset that sometimes settles in during this period. They get these ideas that they are spiritually enlightened and that everyone else is less than they are. They develop spiritual narcissism which INSURES they will not be around people. But this time, instead of it being out of their control, it suddenly feels like now, it is under their control. But it isn't, spiritual narcissism is a telltale sign that the devil of egoic attachments is still present in the psyche. The symptom stays the same, but has simply changed form.

The moment rationalizations form after a Chod session, is a sign there is more work to be done. I call the source of the rationalizations "hungry ghosts". Not unlike the hungry ghosts in Tibetan Lore, the hungry ghosts of the mind are voracious and will do whatever it takes to feed their dysfunction. So when they can't get it directly from you because of Chod, they will do so in another way and in a more covert way as seen above. All this comes from our own unresolved issues in our shadow self.

So please, be mindful of your thoughts after Chod. Is the pain simply changed form? Are you rationalizing? If so, continue the Chod practice until that devil is resolved. It might take a few sessions.

In the next few chapters, we will do a few experiments with Chod that you will not find anywhere else. They are novel, yet very intense and effective.

Let us proceed.

## Experiments in Chod

In the following chapters, we will be altering the Chod process a bit. Instead of severing the devil of egoic attachment from our lives. We will be using our essence to make a direct connection with Buddha's and deities which in turn will sever the antithesis of what these Buddha's represent. I will be using a gentler visualization for most, but not all of these sessions. You can stay with the gentler version or the aggressive one that involves you being torn to shreds, it is up to you.

These exercises will be for specific qualities we may want to enhance in our being. As a reminder, this book is part of my "Baal on Buddhism" series so the entities we use will be from Buddhist tradition, from Tibet and other regions. You can, of course, use this for other traditions if you so please. I, for now, will focus on Buddhism.

**Please note, I go through these sessions quickly in the book, but you are free to prolong these for as long as you like. There is no set rule for how long it should be. I tend to prolong my sessions with Tara since she is one of my patronesses.**

For this book, we will work with six deities and or Buddha's, they are:

**The Goddess Tara for Compassion.**

**The God Mahakala, who is a fiercer equivalent to the Hindu God Shiva. We will use him for Inner strength and power that you can use for anything you desire.**

**The God, Amoghasiddhi, for the attainment of wisdom.**

**The Medicine Buddha, Sangye Menla for healing and becoming the embodiment of healing.**

**The God Kalachakra for protection and the embodiment of protection.**

**The Deity Jambhala for Wealth and Abundance.**

Let us proceed.

## The Goddess Tara - Opening the Heart To Compassion

In this session, we will be looking to acquire compassion in our lives and perhaps even embodying it. We will sever the jadedness and harshness in our hearts and feeding our shadow self to the Goddess of Compassion, Tara. She is one of my patronesses and therefore I wanted to start with her.

Since this is a visual process, you can use the image of Tara I provide in this chapter as your guide or if you have a statue or other image you resonate with, please use that. If you are listening to this book, you can easily find an image online. Study it a bit and when you are asked to visualize her you will have an idea of what to expect. I have several statues of Tara and I use a statue myself.

In this Chod session, we will open our hearts to compassion. Often life makes us jaded and cold. There are so many reasons why this might happen to us. In this Chod session, we will open the heart and allow the infinite compassion of Tara enter our being by feeding and severing our jaded self.

**Now let us go step by step:**

1. Sit with yourself and think of the anger and jadedness that you feel. Has it become a problem for you?
2. Now visualize the Goddess Tara and feel her compassion flow out of her. Look at the image or statue, either in your mind or with your eyes.
3. Now recite her mantra 7 times:

## Om Tare Tuttare Ture Swaha

**(Transliterated: OM TA-RE TOO-TA-RE TOO-RE SWA-HA)**

4. Once the mantra is completed, visualize yourself turning into a mist. See yourself slowly turning into a foggy mist. Now send your mist to Tara and let her drink of it. You can also see your mist go through her third eye. See every last ounce of you enter her. At this point, you are only looking upon her as an observer now.
5. Once you are consumed by her, look at her.
6. Now merge your consciousness with hers. It will be at this point when you will feel the emotional shift. What do you feel?

I know for me personally, I have actually cried when doing this. It moves me so much. I hope it will help you open up.

## The God Mahakala for Inner Strength and Power

In this session, we will be looking to acquire inner strength and power for any purpose you desire. Mahakala is a fierce energy so please be mindful when doing this session. We will be using the more aggressive method of visualization for this session.

Since this is a visual process, you can use the image of Mahakala I provide in this chapter as your guide or if you have a statue or other image you resonate with, please use that. If you are listening to this book, you can easily find an image online. Study it a bit and when you are asked to visualize him you will have an idea of what to expect. I use the image below and a few others when working with Mahakala. I have not yet found a good statue of him that I resonate with.

Image obtained from Wikimedia

In this Chod session, we will look to acquire strength and power from Mahakala. There are so many reasons why we may require such power. You can use it for whatever it is you want.

**Now let us go step by step:**

1. Sit with yourself and think of the need for inner strength and power. Why do you need it?
2. Now visualize Mahakala and feel his strong essence. Look at the image or statue, either in your mind or with your eyes.
3. Now recite his mantra 7 times:

## Om Shri Mahakala Yak Gya Be Ta Li Hum Dza

(Transliterated: OM SHREE MA-HA-KA-LA YAK GYA BE TA LEE HUM DZA)

4. Once the mantra is completed, visualize yourself torn to shreds by wild beasts or spirits. Now See Mahakala consume you. See every last ounce of you enter his mouth. At this point, you are only looking upon him as an observer now.
5. Once you are consumed look at his face.
6. Now merge your consciousness with his. It will be at this point when you will feel the emotional shift. What do you feel?

I love this session. I experimented with this session twice and it kept me up at night. Not out of fear, but I felt this energy run through me. It's very powerful.

# Amoghasiddhi for the Attainment of Wisdom

In this session, we will be looking to acquire wisdom. It can be for any purpose. However, I am thinking this should be used more the attainment of spiritual and occult wisdom. I have never tried it for mundane matters, but I suppose you could try it for those mundane topics that you need guidance on.

Amoghasiddhi is one of the five Buddha's of wisdom in the Vajrayana tradition. He is much beloved and his energy is quite strong. His very name means "He whose achievements are not done in vain". It is for this reason thousands of people recite mantras to him.

Since this is a visual process, you can use the image of Amoghasiddhi I provide in this chapter as your guide or if you have a statue or other image you resonate with, please use that. If you are listening to this book, you can easily find an image online. Study it a bit and when you are asked to visualize him you will have an idea of what to expect. I personally use this image online because there doesn't seem to be good statues of him. I did see a few online on amazon.com but they were astronomically priced and the ones on eBay didn't seem right to me.

Amoghasiddhi - Wikimedia - Wikicommons

In this Chod session, we will look to attain and embody wisdom. I have found that after performing this session, my mind was clearer and my writing was more fluid. I did not get any groundbreaking insight just yet, but I feel something will come of it.

**Now let us go step by step:**

1. Sit with yourself and think of the kind of wisdom you wish to achieve. It is occult in nature? Is it for a specific purpose? Or is just to broaden your horizons?
2. Now visualize Amoghasiddhi and feel his presence. See him seated before you. Look at the image or statue, either in your mind or with your eyes.
3. Now recite his mantra 7 times:

## Om Amoghasiddhi Ah Hum

**(Transliterated: OM A-MO-GAH-SID-HEE AH HUM)**

4. Once the mantra is completed, visualize yourself turning into a green mist. See yourself slowly turning into a foggy green mist. Now send your mist to Amoghasiddhi and see him take it in. At this point, you are only looking upon him as an observer now.
5. Once you are consumed by him, look at him.
6. Now merge your consciousness with his. It will be at this point when you will feel the emotional shift. What do you feel?

I did this session the other day and I loved this subtle buzzing I felt in my head. You can feel it working.

# The Medicine Buddha for the Attainment and Embodiment of Health

In this session, we will be looking to bring health into our lives. As they say "Health, is wealth". Although the following session will be for general embodiment of health, you can use it for a specific purpose as well, if you like.

The Medicine Buddha, or Sangye Menla is often associated with physical healing, but he is also for all manner of conditions. Be it from sicknesses of the soul to a broken toe. He also helps us detach from many of the things that form devils of egoic attachment. I highly recommend the "[Sutra of the Medicine Buddha](#)". You can incorporate many verses there into this practice. For our purposes, however, we will use one of his mantras.

Since this is a visual process, you can use the image of the Medicine Buddha I provide in this chapter as your guide or if you have a statue or other image you resonate with, please use that. If you are listening to this book, you can easily find an image online. Study it a bit and when you are asked to visualize him you will have an idea of what to expect. I personally use this statute that can be found on amazon.com "[Medicine Buddha Collectible Sculpture](#)".

In this Chod session, we will look to attain and embody health and wellness. I think you will find this quite moving when you let the energy sink in.

**Now let us go step by step:**

1. Sit with yourself and think of your health and what it is you want healing for. **You can also do this on behalf of others.**
2. Now visualize The Medicine Buddha and feel his presence. See him seated before you. Look at the image or statue, either in your mind or with your eyes.
3. Now recite his mantra 7 times:

## Om Bekanze Bekanze Maha Bekanze Radza Samungate Soha

(Transliterated: OM BE-KAN-DZE BE-KAN-DZE MA-HA BE-KAN-DZE RA-DZA SA-MUNG-GA-TE SO-HA)

4. Once the mantra is completed, visualize yourself turning into a blue mist. See yourself slowly turning into a foggy blue mist. Now send your mist to The Medicine Buddha and see him take it in. At this point, you are only looking upon him as an observer now.
5. Once you are consumed by him, look at him.
6. Now merge your consciousness with his. It will be at this point when you will feel, perhaps physical sensations. This is okay, just let it go through you.

Thus concludes this session.

## The God Kalachakra – For Protection and the Embodiment of Protection

In this session, we will be looking to bring safety and protection in our lives. Although the following session will be for general embodiment and attainment of protection, you can use it for a specific purpose as well, if you like. This can be protection from anything. Be it from people or from spiritual entities which would also include protection from Hexes and curses.

Kalachakra is somewhat of a mysteries figure. His name means "Wheel of time". He is found in Tantric texts and is known to bestow protection. You can also use him to glean deep Tantric mysteries. You may adapt this session for that purpose if you like. For our purposes, we will use him for protection. He is a bit fierce so we will be using the more aggressive form of visualization for this session.

Since this is a visual process, you can use the image of Kalachakra I provide in this chapter as your guide or if you have a statue or other image you resonate with, please use that. If you are listening to this book, you can easily find an image online. Study it a bit and when you are asked to visualize him you will have an idea of what to expect. I personally use the image below.

In this Chod session, we will look to attain protection. I think you will find this quite powerful.

**Now let us go step by step:**

1. Sit with yourself and think of your need for protection. Is there one reason? Or several, think about them. **You can also do this on behalf of others.**
2. Now visualize The Kalachakra and feel his presence. See him standing before you. Look at the image or statue, either in your mind or with your eyes.
3. Now recite his mantra 7 times:

## Om Ah Hum Hoh Ham Khsah Malavaraya Hum Phat

**(Transliterated:** OM AH HUM HOH HAM KSHAH MA-LA-VA-RA-YA HUM PHAT)

4. Once the mantra is completed, visualize yourself torn to shreds by wild beasts or spirits. Now See Kalachakra consume you. See every last ounce of you enter his mouth. At this point, you are only looking upon him as an observer now.
5. Once you are consumed by him, look at him.
6. Now merge your consciousness with his. It will be at this point that you may feel a burst of energy. However, it is also possible you feel anything at all. This does not mean it is not working.

Thus concludes this session.

## The God Jambhala – For Wealth and Abundance

In this session, we will be looking to bring wealth and abundance in our lives. This is a general session to make yourself resonate with abundance, but one can do this with a specific purpose in mind. I recommend that you keep this more general.

Jambhala is lesser-known, but he is actually an emanation of many very popular deities. He is said to be an emanation of Kubera who is a wealth God in Hinduism. In Tibet Lore he is called Dzambhala. It is the Tibetan mantra that we will be using.

Since this is a visual process, you can use the image of Jambhala / Dzambhala I provide in this chapter as your guide or if you have a statue or other image you resonate with, please use that. If you are listening to this book, you can easily find an image online. Study it a bit and when you are asked to visualize him you will have an idea of what to expect. I personally use the image below since I can't find a statue I resonate with.

In this Chod session, we will look to attain abundance. I think you will find this quite powerful.

**Now let us go step by step:**

1. Sit with yourself and think of your need for wealth and abundance. Is there one reason? Or several, think about them.
2. Now visualize The Jambhala and feel his presence. See him sitting before you. Look at the image or statue, either in your mind or with your eyes.
3. Now recite his mantra 7 times:

## Om Dzambhala Dzalin Draye Soha

**(Transliterated: OM DZAM-BHA-LA DZA-LIN DRA-YE SO-HA)**

4. Once the mantra is completed, visualize yourself turning into a golden mist. Now See Jambhala consume you. See every last ounce of you enter his mouth. At this point, you are only looking upon him as an observer now.
5. Once you are consumed by him, look at him.
6. Now merge your consciousness with his. It will be at this point that you will start to embody the energies to become more abundant. This might come in the way of new ideas, good luck etc.

Thus concludes this session.

## Conclusion

There you have it my friends, I truly hope that this process will help you make the breakthroughs you need. Chod is often made to be much more difficult than it is and I wanted to simplify as much as possible. I do not claim this book to be the end-all-be-all of Chod work, it is just a contribution of my own to the field. I also wanted to introduce novels ways of using this process that other have not yet touched upon. I know this process if very powerful and I feel you will find it very powerful as well.

If you are interested in additional guidance with your Chod work, my friend Akasha coaches people through these sessions. You can find her at https://occultistakasha.com/

Be well my friends, see you soon.

So Mote it Be!

## Want to Enhance Your Chod Practice?

I am not one to promote myself. I like to keep things low-key, but I created a new service that has proven to enhance your rituals and your state of mind and I am very excited about it. As many of you may know, I use Brainwave Entrainment Audios to enhance my writing, my rituals and a lot more. I have been using brainwave products since the 80s. I am using one now as I write this.

I have created hyper-specific Brainwave audios geared to specific spiritual entities. For example, if you call upon the Buddha, I have a specific audio for him. If you work with the Hindus Goddess Lakshmi, I have a Brainwave Audio for her as well.

Please visit: www.occultmindscapes.com

I am adding Audios every week and will have something for everyone and for every tradition. I am only charging $3.95 per audio MP3 download, with steep discounts for multiple purchases.

I think you will LOVE them. My beta testers loved them and I am confident you will find them useful as well.

# About Baal Kadmon

Baal Kadmon is an Author, and Occultist based out of New York City. In addition to the Occult, he is a Religious Scholar, Philosopher and a Historian specializing in Ancient History, Late Antiquity and Medieval History. He has studied and speaks Israeli Hebrew · Classical Hebrew · Ugaritic language · Arabic · Judeo-Aramaic · Syriac (language) · Ancient Greek and Classical Latin.

Baal first discovered his occult calling when he was very young. It was only in his teens, when on a trip to the Middle East that he heeded the call. Several teachers and many decades later he felt ready to share what he has learned.

His teachings are unconventional to say the least. He includes in-depth history in almost all the books he writes, in addition to rituals. He shatters the beloved and idolatrously held notions most occultists hold dear. His pared-down approach to magick is refreshing and is very much needed in a field that is mired by self-important magicians who place more importance on pomp and circumstance rather than on magick. What you learn from Baal is straight forward, with no frills. Magick is about bringing about change or a desired result; Magick is a natural birthright...There is no need to complicate it.

www.baalkadmon.com

www.occultmindscapes.com

**Follow Him on Facebook and other Social Media Sites:**

http://baalkadmon.com/social-media/

# Other Books By The Author

**Organized by date of publication from most recent:**

Durga Mantra Magick: Harnessing The Power of the Divine Protectress

The Talmud - An Occultist Introduction

The Path of the Pendulum

Chod Practice Demystified: Severing the Ties That Bind (Baal on Buddhism Book 2)

Asherah – The Queen of Heaven

Dependent Origination for the Layman

The Watchers And Their Ways

Rabbi Isaac Luria: The Lion of the Kabbalah (Jewish Mystics Book 1)

Circe's Wand: Empowerment | Enchantment | Magick

Ganesha Mantra Magick: Calling Upon The God of New Beginnings

Shiva Mantra Magick: Harnessing The Primordial

Tefillin Magick: Using Tefillin For Magickal Purposes (Jewish Magick Book 1)

Jesus Magick (Bible Magick Book 2)

The Magickal Moment Of Now: The Inner Mind of the Advanced Magician

The Magick Of Lilith: Calling Upon The Great Goddess of The Left Hand Path (Mesopotamian Magick Book 1)

The Magickal Talismans of King Solomon

Mahavidya Mantra Magick: Tap Into the 10 Goddesses of Power

Jinn Magick: How to Bind the Jinn to do Your Bidding

Magick And The Bible: Is Magick Compatible With The Bible? (Bible Magick Book 1)

The Magickal Rites of Prosperity: Using Different Methods To Magickally Manifest Wealth

Lakshmi Mantra Magick: Tap Into The Goddess Lakshmi for Wealth and Abundance In All Areas of Life

Tarot Magick: Harness the Magickal Power of the Tarot

The Quantum Magician: Enhancing Your Magick With A Parallel Life

Tibetan Mantra Magick: Tap Into The Power Of Tibetan Mantras

The 42 Letter Name of God: The Mystical Name Of Manifestation (Sacred Names Book 6)

Tara Mantra Magick: How To Use The Power Of The Goddess Tara

Vedic Magick: Using Ancient Vedic Spells To Attain Wealth

The Daemonic Companion: Creating Daemonic Entities To Do Your Will

Tap Into The Power Of The Chant: Attaining Supernatural Abilities Using Mantras (Supernatural Attainments Series

72 Demons Of The Name: Calling Upon The Great Demons Of The Name (Sacred Names Book 5)

Moldavite Magick: Tap Into The Stone Of Transformation Using Mantras (Crystal Mantra Magick Book 1)

Ouija Board Magick - Archangels Edition: Communicate And Harness The Power Of The Great Archangels

Chakra Mantra Magick: Tap Into The Magick Of Your Chakras (Mantra Magick Series Book 4)

Seed Mantra Magick: Master The Primordial Sounds Of The Universe (Mantra Magick Series Book 3)

The Magick Of Saint Expedite: Tap Into The Truly Miraculous Power Of Saint Expedite (Magick Of The Saints Book 2)

Kali Mantra Magick: Summoning The Dark Powers of Kali Ma (Mantra Magick Series Book 2)

Mary Magick: Calling Forth The Divine Mother For Help (Magick Of The Saints Book 1)

Vashikaran Magick: Learn The Dark Mantras Of Subjugation (Mantra Magick Series Book 1)

The Hidden Names Of Genesis: Tap Into The Hidden Power Of Manifestation (Sacred Names Book 4)

The 99 Names Of Allah: Acquiring the 99 Divine Qualities of God (Sacred Names Book 3)

The 72 Angels Of The Name: Calling On the 72 Angels of God (Sacred Names)

The 72 Names of God: The 72 Keys To Transformation (Sacred Names Book 1)

CPSIA information can be obtained
at www.ICGtesting.com
Printed in the USA
LVHW082140140822
725939LV00025B/939